Ancient Egypt
for Kids

Tray Mead

Table of Contents

Bringing It All Together

114

CHAPTER 1

The Land of Pharaohs

Ancient Egypt is often called the "Land of Pharaohs" because of its rich history and the incredible leaders who helped shape its civilization. This chapter will take you on a journey through Ancient Egypt, focusing on the land along the Nile River. You'll discover how this mighty river was more than just a body of water; it was the heart and soul of Egyptian life. The Nile's geographical features were crucial in transforming Egypt into one of the most remarkable civilizations the world has ever seen.

In this chapter, you'll explore everything from the benefits of the Nile's annual flooding to how it provided natural protection for the people living along its banks. You'll learn about the ingenious ways Egyptians managed their agricultural practices in an arid environment, ensuring they had enough food and resources to thrive. We'll also look at how the Nile was a vital route for transportation and trade, helping connect various parts of Egypt. Finally, we'll delve into how this majestic river influenced every aspect of Egyptian culture, from their myths and religious beliefs to their impressive architectural achievements.

Geographical Location Along the Nile River

The land of Ancient Egypt was deeply tied to the Nile River, which played an essential role in shaping its society and daily life. The river's vital waters provided ancient Egyptians with the necessary resources to build a thriving civilization in a desert environment.

First and foremost, the Nile was a crucial source of fresh water, which is indispensable for any community. The people of Ancient Egypt relied on the Nile for drinking water. Without it, their survival would have been impossible. Moreover, the Nile supplied water for irrigation, enabling the Egyptians to cultivate crops in an otherwise arid landscape. They devised systems like basin irrigation, creating networks of earthen banks and channels to manage the floodwaters effectively, ensuring that the soil remained fertile and ready for planting.

One of the most fascinating aspects of the Nile was its annual flooding, known as inundation. Every year, during late summer, the river overflowed its banks, depositing rich, dark silt over the land. This natural event made the surrounding soil incredibly fertile, perfect for farming. The thick layer of nutrient-rich sediment transformed what could have been barren land into a productive agricultural region, supporting crops such as wheat and barley. This abundance of food not only fed the population but also contributed to the growth and prosperity of Egyptian society.

The Nile's significance extended beyond agriculture. It was also a critical transportation route that connected various parts of Ancient Egypt. The river allowed for the movement of people and goods up and down its length, facilitating trade and communication among different regions. Egyptians became adept boat builders, crafting vessels from papyrus reeds and wood. These boats transported everything from livestock and crops to building materials like stones for constructing pyramids and temples.

The river's importance is further highlighted by how it shaped the Egyptians' view of their world. They saw their land as divided into two distinct regions: Kemet, the "black land" of fertile soil along the Nile, and Deshret, the "red land" of the surrounding deserts. This contrast influenced their mythology and religion, with gods like Hapi, who was associated with the annual flood and fertility, playing prominent roles in their belief system.

In addition to being a lifeline, the Nile provided natural protection. The vast deserts on either side acted as formidable barriers against potential invaders. While other civilizations faced constant threats of warfare, the natural fortifications around Egypt allowed it to develop a more stable and secure environment. This security enabled the Egyptians to focus on advancements in technology, arts, and culture without the frequent disruptions common in other regions.

Another significant advantage of the Nile was its role in unifying Upper and Lower Egypt. The river flowed from south to north, fostering connections between these two areas. It supported the concept of the "Two Lands," symbolizing unity under the rule of the pharaohs. This unity was often depicted in art and architecture, where symbols of both regions were combined, showcasing the strength and cohesion brought about by the Nile.

The Nile also influenced the Egyptians' calendar and agricultural practices. Their year started with Akhet, the season of inundation when the river flooded. This was followed by Peret, the growing season, and Shemu, the harvest season. The regularity of this cycle allowed farmers to plan their activities around the river's behavior, leading to efficient and predictable farming practices.

The Nile's importance is evident not just in practical terms but also in cultural representations. The Egyptians built nilometers—devices for measuring the river's water levels—to predict floods and ensure proper irrigation. This practice shows their deep understanding and dependence on the river's behavior. Additionally, many of their most famous monuments, including temples and pyramids, were constructed near the Nile, emphasizing its central role in their civilization.

Understanding the Nile's impact helps us appreciate how Ancient Egyptians adapted to and thrived in their unique environment. The river was more than just a source of water; it was a fundamental element that influenced every aspect of their lives, from agriculture and transportation to culture and religion. By harnessing its power and resources, they created one of history's most remarkable and enduring civilizations.

Even in modern times, the legacy of the Nile continues. The Aswan High Dam, built in the 20th century, controls the river's flow, providing hydroelectric power and regulating floods. This demonstrates how the relationship between the Nile and the people living along its banks has evolved but remains as vital as ever.

Overview of Egyptian Society and Governance

In Ancient Egypt, the pharaoh was seen not just as a king but as a god in human form. The belief that the pharaoh was a divine ruler meant he had absolute power over everything and everyone in the land. People believed that keeping the pharaoh happy would keep the gods happy, ensuring prosperity and stability. The pharaoh's decisions impacted every aspect of life, from laws to daily activities.

The Egyptian society was organized like a pyramid. At the top stood the pharaoh, followed by the nobles and priests. These individuals enjoyed great wealth and comfort, often living luxurious lives. Nobles held important government posts and earned income from tributes paid to the pharaoh.

Priests were responsible for conducting religious ceremonies and maintaining the favor of the gods. Each town had its own deity, influencing local practices and beliefs.

Beneath the nobles and priests were the soldiers, scribes, and craftsmen. Soldiers played a dual role; they fought in wars and supervised building projects during peace times. Scribes held a critical position because they knew how to read and write, a rare skill in ancient Egypt. They kept government records, which helped in administering the vast empire. Craftsmen such as jewelers, potters, and weavers produced essential goods that contributed to the economy.

Merchants and traders formed the next tier of the social pyramid. These people facilitated trade, ensuring the smooth exchange of goods within Egypt and with neighboring regions. Trade was crucial for obtaining resources not available locally, such as timber and precious metals. The bustling markets were filled with merchants selling everything from food to elaborate jewelry.

At the bottom of the social hierarchy were the farmers and slaves. Farmers worked tirelessly tending fields, raising animals, and constructing grand monuments like pyramids and temples. They paid taxes in the form of grain, which was stored to be used in times of famine. Despite their hard work, farmers lived modestly. Slavery was common, and those captured in wars often became slaves. They performed labor-intensive tasks and had limited rights but were considered an important part of society's workforce.

Religion deeply influenced all layers of society. Egyptians worshipped many gods and goddesses, each overseeing different aspects of life and nature. For example, Ra was the sun god, while Osiris was the god of the afterlife. Religious beliefs shaped laws and everyday routines. The construction of temples and statues showed devotion to these deities, and many rituals were performed to gain their favor. Festivals and ceremonies were frequent, and participation was a community affair.

Occupations in ancient Egypt varied widely and were vital to the civilization's success. Physicians treated ailments with remedies made from herbs, while artists created beautiful murals depicting daily life and religious narratives. Fishermen provided seafood, an essential part of the Egyptian diet.

Even children had roles, often helping their families or learning trades.

The vizier was the pharaoh's right-hand man, overseeing many tasks that the pharaoh could not manage alone. This chief minister ensured that taxes were collected and laws were enforced, making him one of the most powerful officials in the kingdom. Viziers worked closely with scribes, who documented everything meticulously.

Despite the rigid hierarchy, social mobility was possible, albeit rare. Some peasants managed to save enough to send their sons to school, hoping they could become scribes and climb the social ladder. Education was a privilege, and being literate opened doors to higher-ranking jobs within the government.

Life in ancient Egypt was a balance between work, religion, and community. People took pride in their roles, no matter how small. Every job was respected, as each contributed to the greater good of the civilization. Whether crafting intricate jewelry, farming fertile lands along the Nile, or serving in the army, everyone had a part to play.

The governance and structure of ancient Egyptian society reflected the culture and beliefs of the time. The pharaoh's divine status underscored the connection between the earthly realm and the gods. The social hierarchy ensured order and productivity, enabling Egypt to thrive for millennia.

Climate of Egypt

Ancient Egypt's hot and dry climate played a significant role in shaping the lifestyle of its people. The intense heat and the arid environment required the Egyptians to come up with creative solutions to ensure they could sustain their civilization. This section will explore how the climate influenced food production, shelter, clothing, and other aspects of daily life.

One of the most critical areas affected by the climate was food production. Given the lack of rain, ancient Egyptians had to rely heavily on the Nile River for irrigation. They developed innovative agricultural practices, such as basin irrigation, which allowed them to capture and store floodwaters. Farmers dug basins and canals to direct water from the Nile to their fields. They also used tools like the shadoof, a long pole with a bucket on one end, to lift water into irrigation channels. This ingenuity helped them maximize the limited water supply and grow essential crops like wheat, barley, and flax (Food and Agriculture Organization of the United Nations, 2020).

In addition to grains, the Egyptians cultivated fruits and vegetables that required careful management. They grew onions, garlic, radishes, lettuce, and parsley to diversify their diet. Fruit trees, such as date palms and fig trees, were also common, though they needed more complex techniques like manual watering and fertilization. Gardens and orchards were often located away from the fertile floodplain, requiring even more effort to maintain. The reliance on pigeon manure for fertilization highlights how resourceful the Egyptians were in adapting to their environment (Food and Agriculture Organization of the United Nations, 2020).

The hot climate also dictated the design of shelters and choice of clothing. Homes were built with materials like mud bricks, which provided natural insulation against the heat. Thick walls and small windows helped keep interiors cool. Roofs were often flat, allowing residents to sleep outside during particularly sweltering nights. Clothing was designed for comfort in high temperatures. Lightweight linen, made from locally grown flax, was the primary fabric. Men typically wore simple kilts, while women donned straight dresses with shoulder straps. Children and laborers sometimes wore little or no clothing to stay comfortable in the heat.

Deserts surrounding the Nile Valley played a crucial role in both protection and daily life. The vast expanses of the Sahara desert acted as natural barriers, deterring invasions from potential enemies. This isolation enabled Egyptian civilization to develop relatively free from constant external threats (Ancient Egypt, n.d.). However, the deserts weren't just obstacles; they were also vital resources. Quarries in the desert provided stone for building monuments and temples. Mining operations extracted valuable minerals like gold and copper, contributing to Egypt's wealth and trade.

Despite the challenging climate, Egypt's strategic location facilitated trade with neighboring regions. The Nile River offered a natural highway for transporting goods. Winds from the north allowed sailboats to travel south, while the river's current carried them northwards. This efficient transportation system enabled Egyptians to trade surplus crops, pottery, and crafted goods for exotic items and raw materials not found locally. Relationships with distant cultures brought new ideas and technologies to Egypt, further enriching their civilization. For instance, through trade, Egyptians adopted fruits like grapes, olives, and pomegranates, broadening their agricultural palette (Ancient Egypt, n.d.).

Understanding the impact of the climate on ancient Egyptian life helps us appreciate their resilience and ingenuity. Despite harsh conditions, they developed a thriving society. Their successful adaptation to the environment demonstrates the profound influence geography can have on culture and societal development.

To help young readers visualize these concepts, a fun activity involving a simple map tracing of the Nile and surrounding areas can be introduced. Kids can actively engage in the learning process by recognizing key landmarks that played a role in Ancient Egypt. Encouraging children to visualize geography reinforces their understanding of the subject matter. This friendly competition can spark discussions about travel, exploration, and geography in real life.

Summary and Reflections

In this chapter, we've journeyed through the wonders of Ancient Egypt, discovering how the Nile River was the heartbeat of this fascinating civilization. From providing essential water for drinking and farming to acting as a highway for trade and travel, the Nile was truly a lifeline. The river's annual floods brought fertile soil perfect for growing crops, and its natural defenses offered protection from invaders, allowing Egypt to flourish. We also glimpsed how the god-like status of the pharaohs and a well-structured society contributed to their remarkable achievements.

We've also explored how Egypt's climate shaped daily life, from the foods they grew to the shelters they built. Ingenious irrigation systems and farming techniques ensured survival in an arid landscape, while homes provided cool retreats from the scorching sun. Their strategic location helped them trade with nearby regions, bringing new ideas and goods into their culture. Altogether, understanding the geography and environment of Ancient Egypt helps us see how resourceful and inventive its people were, creating one of history's most enduring civilizations.

CHAPTER 2

The Mighty Pharaohs

Exploring the lives of the mighty pharaohs is like stepping into an ancient world filled with grandeur and mystery. These rulers were not just kings and queens but also seen as gods on earth, wielding immense power and influence over their people. From the splendor of King Tutankhamun's treasures to the groundbreaking reign of Hatshepsut, each pharaoh left a unique mark on history that continues to captivate our imagination. They built magnificent structures, led armies, and shaped the culture and religion of Ancient Egypt in ways that still resonate today.

In this chapter, you will journey through the fascinating lives and achievements of some of the most famous pharaohs. You'll learn how King Tut navigated leadership at a young age and restored traditional beliefs to his kingdom. Discover how Hatshepsut broke barriers as a female ruler and contributed to Egypt's prosperity through her innovative trade expeditions and architectural masterpieces. By examining their stories, we gain insight into the incredible civilization of Ancient Egypt and the lasting legacies these mighty pharaohs left behind.

Reign of King Tutankhamun

King Tutankhamun, often referred to affectionately as King Tut, is one of the most famous pharaohs of Ancient Egypt. His story is remarkable, especially considering he became pharaoh at a very young age. Tutankhamun ascended the throne when he was just about nine or ten years old. Imagine becoming a king while still being a kid! His youth and inexperience presented challenges, but he managed to navigate leadership during a significant period for Egypt.

During his reign, Egypt was recovering from religious turmoil. Before King Tut, there was a time when the old gods were abandoned in favor of worshipping only one god, Aten. This religious upheaval caused considerable unrest among the people. When King Tut became pharaoh, he worked towards restoring traditional beliefs and practices. This return to the old ways brought stability back to the kingdom, showing how important it is for leaders to understand and respect their people's traditions and faiths.

But what makes King Tut even more fascinating is not just his life as a ruler but what was discovered thousands of years after his death. In 1922, British archaeologist Howard Carter unearthed King Tut's tomb in the Valley of the Kings. This discovery was monumental because the tomb was nearly intact, filled with treasures that glittered like the stars. Among the artifacts were golden chariots, intricately carved statues, and the famous golden death mask of Tutankhamun himself.

These treasures weren't just pretty objects. They told us stories about what life was like in ancient Egypt. The golden mask, for instance, was crafted with such detail that it revealed the advanced skills of Egyptian artisans. The items found in the tomb gave us a glimpse into the wealth and splendor that surrounded the pharaohs. There were also everyday items, like board games and food containers, which showed us what kinds of games they played and what they ate.

One of the most intriguing aspects of the tomb's contents is how they reflect ancient Egyptian beliefs about the afterlife. Egyptians believed in a life after death where the dead would need all the comforts of their earthly existence. This is why King Tut's tomb was packed with goodies — to ensure he had everything he needed to live comfortably in the afterlife.

The discovery of King Tut's tomb sparked a global fascination with ancient Egypt. Movies, books, and exhibitions have brought his story to life for millions of people around the world. For example, the iconic 1932 film "The Mummy" was inspired by the tales of curses linked to King Tut's tomb. Exhibits showcasing the treasures of Tutankhamun have traveled across continents, drawing large crowds eager to see the glimmering relics firsthand.

Moreover, King Tut has become a cultural icon in contemporary times. From Halloween costumes to references in pop culture, his legacy continues to capture the imagination of young and old alike. Modern-day explorers and history enthusiasts remain intrigued by the mystery surrounding his brief life and untimely death.

In addition to movies and exhibits, literature has greatly contributed to keeping King Tut's memory alive. Many children's books have been written about him, making his story accessible and engaging for young readers. These accounts often highlight the excitement of discovery and the adventure that comes with exploring ancient history.

Furthermore, the legends and lore surrounding King Tut's supposed curse have added an element of mystery and excitement. While scientists dismiss these curses as myths, they add a layer of thrill to his story. Stories of those who entered his tomb and met with mysterious fates intrigue and captivate audiences, adding spice to historical facts.

King Tutankhamun's story is indeed a captivating chapter in the rich tapestry of Ancient Egypt. His rise to power as a child, his efforts to restore order, and the magnificent treasures buried with him offer immense insight into this incredible civilization. Through the discovery of his tomb, we have learned so much about the daily life, artistry, and spiritual beliefs of ancient Egyptians.

Hatshepsut: The Female Pharaoh

Hatshepsut was one of the most remarkable figures in ancient Egyptian history, not only because she was a successful pharaoh but also because she was a woman who ruled in a man's world. In a time when leadership roles were almost exclusively held by men, Hatshepsut broke societal norms by assuming the title and role of pharaoh. By doing so, she challenged the traditional views of leadership and set an extraordinary example for future generations.

Taking up the role of pharaoh was no small feat. Hatshepsut did not just take on the title; she embraced it wholeheartedly, even adopting male attire and wearing the false beard traditionally associated with kings. This was not merely a costume choice but a bold statement about her authority and determination to be seen as equal to any male ruler. Her reign demonstrated that leadership qualities were not confined to gender, paving the way for more inclusive views on who can lead a nation.

One of Hatshepsut's most significant achievements was the construction of her mortuary temple at Deir el-Bahari, which still stands today as a symbol of her ingenuity and vision. This magnificent structure is not just an architectural wonder; it has sparked interest in engineering and the arts for centuries. The temple's design is unique, with its terraced levels and grand colonnades, setting it apart from other monuments of the time. It served multiple purposes: a place of worship, a site for ceremonies, and a final resting place for the queen.

The grandeur of this temple highlighted Hatshepsut's commitment to celebrating both divine and royal power. But beyond its religious importance, the temple has inspired countless architects and artists throughout history. Its innovative design elements have been studied extensively, contributing significantly to our understanding of ancient Egyptian architecture. Young engineers and artists can look at this structure and find inspiration in its beauty and complexity, understanding the impact of creative thinking and advanced planning.

Hatshepsut's reign wasn't marked only by monumental buildings; it was also a time of prosperity and expansion. One of her key strategies for strengthening Egypt was expanding its trade networks. She sent trading expeditions to far-off lands like Punt, which brought back valuable goods such as gold, ebony, and incense. These trade missions increased Egypt's wealth and influence, showcasing how economies thrive through connections with others.

The expansion of these trade networks had far-reaching effects. Not only did they bring material wealth to Egypt, but they also facilitated cultural exchanges that enriched

Egyptian society. People learned about new technologies, artistic styles, and even culinary practices from distant lands. This period of economic growth and cultural enrichment underscores the importance of trade in building strong, prosperous nations. Kids learning about Hatshepsut can see how crucial it is to establish and maintain good relationships with people from different places.

Modern archaeologists have played a crucial role in resurrecting Hatshepsut's legacy, teaching us the importance of archaeology and historical recovery. For many years, her accomplishments were overshadowed or forgotten, mainly because subsequent male rulers tried to erase her memory. Statues were defaced, inscriptions were chiseled away, and her name was omitted from king lists. However, determined archaeologists uncovered artifacts and studied ancient texts that revealed the true extent of her achievements.

By piecing together fragments of the past, archaeologists have brought Hatshepsut back into the spotlight. Their work teaches us valuable lessons about the importance of preserving history and understanding our heritage. It's a reminder that history is not just about famous names and dates but about uncovering the stories of those who have shaped our world. Kids can learn that every fragment of pottery or piece of inscription holds a clue to the past, and through careful discovery and analysis, we can reconstruct stories long buried by time.

Historical Impact and Legacy of Pharaohs

Pharaohs were central to the life and culture of Ancient Egypt. They weren't just powerful rulers; they were seen as gods on earth. This divine status helped them establish and maintain the cultural and religious practices that defined Egyptian society. From rituals performed at temples to grand public festivals, pharaohs played a key role in ensuring that these traditions continued for centuries. Their influence extended beyond their lifetimes through the stories, myths, and customs that remain subjects of fascination today.

One of the most striking ways pharaohs have left their mark is through their monumental constructions. The pyramids, towering above the sands of Giza, are perhaps the best-known examples. These incredible structures were not only tombs but also symbols of the pharaohs' eternal power and the architectural skill of their time. Building such massive monuments required immense resources and labor, reflecting the pharaoh's ability to mobilize an entire nation. Temples like Karnak and Luxor stand as testament to their devotion to the gods and their ability to create awe-inspiring wonders. The intricate carvings and vast columns showcase artistic achievements that continue to inspire awe among visitors and scholars alike.

Studying the pharaohs provides us with valuable insights into ancient governance, social structures, and economic systems. Ancient Egypt was one of the first great civilizations to develop a centralized government, with the pharaoh at its head. This form of leadership influenced later societies and set patterns that can be traced through history. The way pharaohs managed resources, from the Nile's precious waters to the sprawling fields of grain, shows a sophisticated understanding of economy and sustainability. Exploring their reigns helps historians understand how laws were enforced, how taxes were collected, and how projects were organized—a fascinating glimpse into the early complexities of state management.

Pharaohs also had to navigate complex social hierarchies. At the top stood the pharaoh, followed by nobles, priests, scribes, artisans, and farmers. The social structure was rigid, yet each level had a crucial role in maintaining the kingdom's stability. For example, priests conducted vital religious ceremonies, while scribes recorded important events and transactions. This system ensured that the society functioned smoothly, revealing an advanced level of organization that is impressive even by today's standards.

The legacy of the pharaohs continues to captivate and inspire people around the world. Modern culture has embraced these ancient rulers in books, movies, and exhibitions, bringing their stories to life for new generations. Characters like Cleopatra and Ramses II have become icons, representing bravery, intelligence, and grandeur. These portrayals keep the memory of Ancient Egypt alive, fueling imaginations and sparking interest in history and archaeology.

Pharaohs often appear in popular media, influencing everything from fashion to architecture. Movies set in Ancient Egypt feature stunning visuals inspired by historical artifacts and buildings. Fashion designers sometimes borrow elements from Egyptian art and clothing, creating styles that echo the past. Even video games set in ancient times allow players to experience what life might have been like under the rule of a pharaoh. These modern interpretations help keep the legacy of the pharaohs vibrant and relevant.

In addition to entertainment, the influence of pharaohs permeates educational content. Schools and museums around the world teach about Ancient Egypt, using the lives and achievements of the pharaohs as a focal point. Exhibitions featuring mummies, jewelry, and artifacts draw crowds eager to learn more about these legendary figures. Educational programs often include interactive components, allowing children to engage with history in hands-on ways. These experiences foster a deeper appreciation for the achievements of Ancient Egypt and the lasting impact of its rulers.

Pharaohs have contributed greatly to the field of archaeology. The treasures found in tombs, such as those discovered in the Valley of the Kings, provide invaluable information about ancient life. Objects like pottery, tools, and clothing offer clues about daily activities, trade networks, and technological advancements. The careful study of these items helps archaeologists piece together the puzzle of ancient Egyptian civilization. Each discovery adds to our understanding of how the pharaohs lived, how they ruled, and how they interacted with other cultures.

The pharaohs' ability to mobilize resources for monumental projects highlights their strategic planning and organizational skills. For instance, constructing enormous structures like the Great Pyramid required precise engineering and extensive manpower. The logistics involved—quarrying stone, transporting materials, and coordinating labor—demonstrate a high level of competence. These achievements not only symbolize the pharaohs' power but also reflect their capability to execute complex plans efficiently.

Moreover, the riches buried with pharaohs, such as gold masks and intricate jewelry, reveal their wealth and the importance they placed on the afterlife. These burial practices show a deep connection to religious beliefs and the desire to ensure a successful journey to the next world. The artistry of these treasures also showcases the advanced skills of ancient craftsmen, who created exquisite pieces that continue to dazzle viewers thousands of years later.

Final Insights

This chapter introduced us to the incredible lives and achievements of some of Ancient Egypt's most famous pharaohs. From the fascinating story of King Tutankhamun's young reign and the treasures found in his tomb, to Hatshepsut's groundbreaking rule as a female pharaoh who defied gender norms, we've explored how these leaders shaped their world and left an enduring legacy. Their monumental constructions, innovative leadership, and efforts to restore stability offer us valuable insights into the complexities and brilliance of ancient Egyptian civilization.

As we wrap up this chapter, it's clear that the pharaohs were not only rulers but also visionaries whose actions have inspired generations. The stories of their lives, the splendor of their achievements, and the mysteries surrounding their reigns continue to captivate minds today. Whether through grand temples, intricate artifacts, or tales of discovery, these legendary figures have made an indelible mark on history. And as we dig deeper into their legacies, we uncover lessons about leadership, culture, and perseverance that still resonate with us today.

CHAPTER 3

Secrets of the Afterlife

Exploring the afterlife was a big part of Ancient Egyptian culture. Their beliefs about what happened after death were deeply rooted in rituals and practices that might sound strange to us today. Mummification, for example, was not just about preserving the body; it was a highly spiritual process that took great care and skill. The Egyptians developed special techniques using oils and natural salts to keep the body looking lifelike, believing this helped the deceased have a better journey beyond death.

In this chapter, we'll dive deep into these fascinating traditions. You'll learn all about the detailed process of mummification, from washing and embalming the body to wrapping it up in linen strips with protective amulets tucked inside. We'll also explore the importance of the Book of the Dead, a guide filled with spells and instructions to help navigate the challenges of the underworld. By understanding these rituals and texts, we can uncover the rich spiritual life of the Egyptians and see how much effort they put into ensuring a safe passage to the afterlife.

The Process of Mummification

Mummification was a fascinating and complex process that played a crucial role in Ancient Egyptian beliefs about the afterlife. To prepare for the journey beyond death, Egyptians developed intricate methods to preserve the body using special oils and drying techniques. This careful preservation was essential as they believed it helped the deceased navigate the afterlife.

The elaborate process of mummification typically took around 70 days. It began with embalming, where the body was carefully washed and purified. Embalming included the removal of internal organs, such as the brain, which was extracted through the nostrils using long hooks. This step prevented the body from decaying too quickly. The other organs, including the lungs, liver, stomach, and intestines, were removed through an incision on the left side of the body. These organs were then placed in canopic jars, each guarded by a deity of protection.

One organ often left inside the body was the heart because it was believed to be the seat of one's thoughts and feelings. Egyptians thought the heart would be weighed against the feather of Ma'at, the goddess of truth and justice, to determine one's fate in the afterlife. After the organs were removed, the body cavities were cleaned and packed with natron, a natural salt, to dry out the flesh completely.

Once the drying process was complete, the body was washed again and wrapped in linen strips. The wrapping itself held significant spiritual meaning. Priests conducted rituals and recited prayers to protect the deceased from evil spirits. Amulets and talismans were placed between the layers of linen to provide additional protection and guidance for the journey ahead. Some funerary texts, like spells written on papyrus, were also incorporated into the wrappings.

Burying objects with the mummy reflected the individual's belief system and their status in society. Tombs of wealthy individuals or royalty, such as pharaohs, often contained valuable items like jewelry, food, and furniture, all intended to be used in the afterlife. For instance, Tutankhamun's tomb, one of the most famous discoveries, was filled with treasures that showcased his wealth and prepared him for the afterlife. His well-preserved mummy offers an intimate look at the personal connections between history and individuals.

Mummies have always intrigued us, partly due to myths and legends that surround them. Stories of walking mummies or curses have spurred fascination and fear for centuries. However, most of these tales are products of imagination rather than fact. Real-life mummies, like those of Tutankhamun and Sety I, show no evidence of such supernatural occurrences. Instead, they stand as remarkable records of ancient practices and beliefs.

Understanding the mummification process dispels many misconceptions about these ancient customs. For example, the methodical extraction and preservation techniques counter the idea of crude or primitive methods. In reality, the mummification process was a highly sophisticated art, refined over thousands of years.

Some of the earliest mummies discovered in Egypt date back to the Predynastic period (c.5500-3100 BCE). These early mummies were often naturally preserved by the desert's heat and sand. This natural preservation likely inspired the development of deliberate mummification practices, aligning with evolving religious and afterlife beliefs.

By studying mummies and the artifacts buried with them, archaeologists have gained invaluable insights into Ancient Egyptian culture. They help us understand the daily lives, social hierarchies, and spiritual practices of people who lived thousands of years ago.

The Book of the Dead and Its Importance

In ancient Egypt, an important text called the Book of the Dead played a crucial role in guiding the souls of the dead through the afterlife. Unlike modern books with a single author, this was a collection of spells and instructions written by many scribes, each version unique to its owner. These texts were often placed in tombs, sometimes on papyrus scrolls or inscribed on the walls of the burial chamber, to help the deceased navigate the challenges they would face in the underworld.

One key function of the Book of the Dead was to protect the deceased from dangers and assist them in overcoming obstacles. The spells included in these texts were tailored to individuals, ensuring that the instructions were specific to their journey. Some spells were so essential that they appeared frequently across different copies of the book. For example, Spell 17 discussed the importance of the sun-god Re (also called Ra), highlighting how vital the divine was to Egyptian beliefs about life after death. Another common spell involved naming various parts of a doorway before passing through, which showed just how detailed and specialized these instructions could be. Each book might also contain illustrations, making it accessible even to those who couldn't read hieroglyphs but could understand pictures.

One of the most fascinating ceremonies described in the Book of the Dead is the Weighing of the Heart. According to this belief, when a person died, their heart was weighed against the feather of Maat, the goddess of truth and justice. This ceremony determined whether the person's soul was pure enough to enter the afterlife. If the heart weighed less than the feather, it meant the person had lived a truthful life and was allowed to join the gods. However, if it was heavier, the heart would be devoured by a fearsome creature called Ammit, resulting in the soul's destruction. This vivid imagery, often found in the Book of the Dead, helped convey the importance of honesty during one's lifetime and the consequences of one's actions.

Modern archaeologists continue to study the Book of the Dead, translating the texts to gain deeper insights into ancient Egyptian beliefs and practices. These ancient documents provide a window into how the

Egyptians viewed life, death, and the afterlife. They reveal not only the religious significance of mummification but also the broader cultural context, such as the roles of various gods and the Egyptians' understanding of the soul. The ka and ba were thought to be aspects of the soul that lived on after death, with the ka requiring a physical form, like a mummy, to return to. This connection between the Book of the Dead and mummification highlights the intricate and deeply spiritual nature of Egyptian funerary practices.

Archaeological discoveries of different versions of the Book of the Dead have allowed scholars to trace the evolution of these texts over time. The oldest known funerary writings, the Pyramid Texts, were originally reserved for royalty. Later, these evolved into the Coffin Texts, which were more accessible to non-royals, and eventually into the Book of the Dead during the New Kingdom period. By examining these variations, researchers can observe changes in religious beliefs and practices across centuries. The ongoing translation and interpretation work mean that our understanding of these fascinating texts is constantly evolving, adapting to new findings and perspectives.

Interestingly, the Book of the Dead has also influenced modern culture, often romanticized in movies and literature. One well-known example is the film "The Mummy," which, despite its entertaining storyline, doesn't accurately represent the true nature of these ancient texts (Warren, 2023). By studying the real Book of the Dead, Egyptologists aim to preserve and share a more accurate understanding of the Egyptian view of the afterlife. This helps dispel myths and misconceptions while enriching our appreciation of an ancient civilization's profound spiritual legacy.

The Book of the Dead's spells were not only practical guidelines for the deceased but also reflections of personal desires and fears. Each version of the book was customized, sometimes with blank spaces left for names to be added later. This bespoke approach ensured that every individual's journey through the afterlife was as smooth and secure as possible. The care and detail put into these texts underscore the importance the ancient Egyptians placed on preparing for the afterlife.

For young readers today, learning about the Book of the Dead provides a fascinating glimpse into how ancient people understood life and death. It reveals a world where magic, religion, and daily life were deeply intertwined, showing how much effort people put into ensuring a safe passage to the next world. The vibrant images and detailed spells offer a tangible connection to the past, making the topic both engaging and educational.

The role of archaeologists in unearthing and interpreting these texts cannot be overstated. Their work involves meticulously piecing together fragments of papyrus and deciphering ancient symbols to build a coherent picture of Egyptian funerary practices. This research not only enriches our knowledge of history but also sparks curiosity and wonder about how people lived thousands of years ago.

Famous Mummies and Their Stories

When we think about ancient Egypt, one of the most fascinating topics is mummies. Famous mummies like Tutankhamun give us a look into ancient burial practices and beliefs. Tutankhamun, often called King Tut, was an Egyptian pharaoh who died young. His tomb, filled with treasures and well-preserved artifacts, was discovered by Howard Carter in 1922. This discovery provided incredible insights into how the Egyptians prepared for the afterlife.

One key aspect of these findings is the rich burial goods placed alongside Tutankhamun. These items were meant to help him in the afterlife – from golden chariots to intricate jewelry. The care with which his body was preserved also tells us a lot about the importance of the afterlife in ancient Egyptian culture. They believed that preserving the body was crucial for the deceased's soul to survive and enjoy the afterlife.

But how were these mummies so well-preserved? This brings us to the interesting conditions behind better-preserved mummies. Methods varied over time, but common techniques included using natron, a type of salt that dried out the body. Embalmers removed internal organs, which were prone to decay, and treated the body with oils and resins that had antibacterial properties. Over time, embalmers perfected their skills, leading to better-preserved mummies (Arnold, 2020).

The diversity in preservation methods also reflected social status. Royal figures like Tutankhamun received elaborate treatments, while common folks often underwent simpler processes. The quality of materials and the expertise of embalmers available to them played a significant role in the condition of the mummies that have been discovered. For example, some mummified animals found in tombs, such as cats and birds, were preserved using simpler techniques compared to those used for pharaohs (Smithsonian, 2012).

The stories behind these famous mummies create a personal connection to history. Each mummy tells a tale of who they were, their social status, and how they were treated after death. Tutankhamun's youth and mysterious death make his story captivating. Another mummy, Ramses II, known as Ramses the Great, lived well into his nineties and was a powerful ruler. His mummy shows signs of arthritis and dental issues, giving us glimpses into his life and health.

These tales reveal more than just the lives of individuals; they provide a broader picture of ancient Egyptian society. The elaborate burial practices for pharaohs highlight the immense respect and resources devoted to ensuring their safe passage to the afterlife. On the other hand, more modest burials reflect the everyday experiences of common people. Looking at both ends of this spectrum provides a comprehensive understanding of the social hierarchies and values of ancient Egypt.

An important part of the journey to understanding mummies involves examining mummification myths. Many popular myths, like walking mummies or curses, stem from fictional representations rather than historical accuracy. For instance, the "curse of the mummy" linked to the opening of Tutankhamun's tomb was largely sensationalized by the media. While several individuals involved in the excavation did die under mysterious circumstances, there's no substantial evidence to support the existence of a curse.

Instead, the actual process of mummification was a meticulous and sacred practice grounded in religious beliefs. Ancient Egyptians believed that preserving the body was essential for the deceased's spirit to return and receive offerings. This belief in the ka, ba, and akh spirits explains why such efforts were made to ensure the body remained intact. The ka would stay in the tomb, the ba could fly outside, and the akh traveled through the Underworld to reach final judgment (Smithsonian, 2012).

Refuting these myths helps us appreciate the true significance of mummification. It's more than a spooky story; it's a testament to the deep spiritual and cultural values held by the Egyptians. In understanding these practices, we gain a clearer and more respectful view of their worldview and rituals surrounding death and the afterlife.

Closing Remarks

Ancient Egyptians believed mummification was essential for navigating the afterlife. They carefully preserved bodies using intricate methods, like removing and storing organs in special jars. The heart, which they thought held thoughts and feelings, stayed inside to be weighed against a feather to judge one's truthfulness. By drying and wrapping the body with linens, they protected it from evil spirits and prepared it for the journey ahead. This process, combined with placing valuable items in tombs, reflected their deep connection between the earthly life and the afterlife.

The Book of the Dead added another layer to these beliefs, guiding souls through the underworld with spells and instructions specific to each person. These texts ensured that the deceased could overcome any obstacles on their journey. By studying these fascinating documents and the mummies themselves, archaeologists have learned about the ancient Egyptians' spiritual practices and daily lives. Their work has helped us understand how the rich tapestry of religious beliefs influenced every aspect of Egyptian culture, making it clear that they took great care to ensure a safe and successful passage to the afterlife.

CHAPTER 4

Daily Life in Ancient Egypt

Daily life in ancient Egypt was incredibly rich and varied, offering a fascinating glimpse into how people lived thousands of years ago. From their earliest days, children were an essential part of Egyptian society, contributing to both family and community life. The roles they played, the chores they did, and even the games they engaged in all shaped them into responsible members of society. Their education, whether learning complex hieroglyphs or mastering household skills, set the foundation for a future that would carry on the traditions and responsibilities of their ancestors. Meanwhile, religious festivals provided not just spiritual enrichment but also opportunities for communal bonding, with children playing active roles in these significant events.

In this chapter, we'll dive deep into the daily lives of ancient Egyptian children, revealing how they balanced responsibilities with play. Discover what boys and girls learned at a young age, how they helped their families through various chores, and the kinds of games that sparked their creativity. We'll also explore the types of foods that nourished them and the intricate clothing customs that adorned them. Get ready to journey back in time and uncover the vibrant and interwoven fabric of everyday existence in one of history's most captivating civilizations!

Roles and Responsibilities of Children

Children played an essential role in the family and society of ancient Egypt. Their contributions were vital to maintaining daily life and ensuring the smooth functioning of their communities. Let's dive into how these young Egyptians made a difference through their education, chores, games, and participation in religious festivals.

In ancient Egypt, education was highly valued. Starting from a young age, children learned to read and write, often practicing hieroglyphs on pottery shards or limestone flakes. Boys from wealthier families attended school, where they studied various subjects, including reading, writing, mathematics, and sometimes even accounting. These skills were particularly important because being literate opened many doors for future careers, especially in governmental and administrative positions. Since many trades required literacy, knowledge became a key asset passed down to ensure the family's prosperity and societal contribution.

Girls, though less frequently formally educated than boys, still received valuable instruction. Many learned the art of weaving, embroidery, and managing household finances from their mothers. This practical education was crucial as it prepared them for their roles within the household and equipped them with skills that could contribute to the family's economic stability. While formal schooling wasn't as common for girls, their informal education was equally significant in maintaining the day-to-day functions of a household.

Responsibilities were also part of daily life for ancient Egyptian children. From a very young age, they were given specific chores that taught them responsibility and the importance of contributing to the family unit. Boys might help with agricultural tasks, learning to plant, irrigate, and harvest crops. Girls often assisted with cooking, grinding grain, and caring for younger siblings. These chores instilled a sense of discipline and work ethic, making children feel capable and valued within the family structure.

Games and play were not just a way to pass time; they played a critical role in fostering creativity and social interactions among children. Common games included wrestling, which built physical strength and skill, and board games like Senet, which required strategic thinking and patience. Children also played with simple toys such as dolls, balls, and spinning tops. Through these activities, they developed important social skills like teamwork and fair play, preparing them for adult responsibilities and community participation.

Religious festivals were a major aspect of life in ancient Egypt, and children were actively involved in these cultural events. They often participated in processions, carrying small statues or other sacred objects. During these festivals, they learned about their gods and goddesses and the significance of religious rituals. This involvement helped instill a strong sense of cultural identity and spiritual awareness in the young members of society. By participating in these communal events, children understood their place within the larger social fabric and contributed to preserving cultural traditions.

Food Customs

The ancient Egyptians had rich and varied dietary habits that were more than just about eating good food. What they ate was closely tied to their daily life, culture, and even their spirituality.

One of the staples of the Egyptian diet was bread. Made from emmer wheat or barley, bread was essential for every meal. There were different varieties, ranging from flatbreads to conical loaves, each baked in clay ovens or over open fires. Alongside bread, beer was another daily fixture. Unlike modern beers, ancient Egyptian beer was thick and cloudy, made from fermented barley bread. It was nutritious and often used as a form of payment or ration for workers, ensuring not just sustenance but also societal functioning (Oppenheim, 2015).

Vegetables, too, played a crucial role in their meals. Ancient Egyptians grew a variety of vegetables such as onions, garlic, leeks, lentils, and cucumbers. These were either consumed raw, cooked, or preserved for later use. Fruits like dates, figs, grapes, and pomegranates added sweetness to their diet. Interestingly, dates and honey were especially significant during celebrations, symbolizing sweetness and festivity. Honey wasn't just a sweet treat; it was also used in religious rituals and offerings.

Fish was another important component of their diet. The Nile River provided a plentiful supply of fish such as catfish, perch, and tilapia. Fish was often dried or salted to preserve it for future consumption. However, it was considered a luxury item that not everyone could afford regularly.

Certain foods were reserved for special occasions or rituals. Meat, for instance, was more commonly associated with feasts and religious ceremonies. Beef, poultry, and game birds were usually served at banquets or offered to the gods. Goose and duck meat were delicacies enjoyed by the wealthy and during festivals. On rare occasions, pharaohs and high-ranking officials were buried with food items, including meat, to ensure they had sustenance in the afterlife (Halawa, 2023).

Ancient Egyptians didn't just eat to live; they also believed deeply in the spiritual importance of food. They thought that their gods needed nourishment, just like humans. Religious rituals often included food offerings, which could range from simple bread and beer to elaborate meals featuring meat and fruits. This connection between food and spirituality meant that what they ate was imbued with meaning beyond mere survival (Oppenheim, 2015).

Food was central to social gatherings and celebrations. Festivals often featured large feasts where communities came together to enjoy an abundance of food. These events were not only a time to indulge but also a way to strengthen community ties and cultural identity. For example, during the Opet Festival, which honored the god Amun, people would gather for days of feasting and revelry, showcasing their culinary traditions.

Sweet treats were not just limited to festivals. Everyday sweets included dates, honey, and sometimes cakes made with flour and sweetened with fruit juice or honey. These sugary delights were not just enjoyed by the elite but were accessible to most citizens, reflecting a shared cultural appreciation for sweetness.

The tools and methods used for cooking were quite advanced for their time. Egyptians had pottery and metal cookware, and they employed various methods like baking, roasting, boiling, and frying. Food preparation was a communal activity, often involving family members working together to prepare daily meals or special feasts. Men typically took on cooking roles in temples and during large-scale food preparations, while women managed household cooking and preservation duties.

Their diverse diet also showcased their resourcefulness and understanding of agriculture. Seasonal variations influenced what was available, yet they managed to cultivate a variety of crops year-round. Techniques like irrigation ensured they could grow enough food to sustain their population even in challenging conditions.

The impact of their diet extended beyond immediate needs. The types of food consumed influenced their health and lifestyle. A diet rich in vegetables, bread, and occasionally meat likely contributed to their physical endurance, necessary for the labor-intensive tasks many Egyptians performed, such as building pyramids or farming.

Moreover, their dietary habits provide a window into the economic structure of ancient Egypt. The distribution and access to certain foods, like meat and fish, highlighted social hierarchies. Wealthier individuals had more varied diets, while the poor relied mainly on bread and vegetables. This disparity underscores the broader social dynamics at play in ancient Egyptian society.

Visiting historical sites and examining artifacts show us how integrated food was in their lives. Tomb paintings, for example, frequently depict scenes of food preparation, farming, and feasting, emphasizing its cultural significance. These visual records serve as a testament to the centrality of food in their everyday life and spiritual practices.

Clothing Customs

Ancient Egyptians were known for their unique and practical clothing styles, which were well-suited to their hot climate. Nearly everyone, regardless of social status, wore garments made from linen, a fabric spun from the fibers of the flax plant. Linen was strong, breathable, and comfortable, making it ideal for the sweltering temperatures in Egypt. The natural color of linen was white, but wealthier individuals sometimes managed to add colors for a bit of flair.

Men typically wore kilts, which were skirts that wrapped around their bodies and were tied with belts. These kilts were not only cool and comfortable but also allowed for ease of movement. Wealthy men flaunted lighter-weight, higher-quality linen kilts that were often more finely pleated and adorned with embroidery. For the everyday man, a kilt provided a simple yet effective way to beat the heat while going about daily tasks.

Women, on the other hand, wore long dresses that fit closely to their bodies. These dresses were usually held up by one or two shoulder straps, leaving the shoulders bare, which added to the comfort in the hot climate. Some wealthy women even wore dresses made entirely from beads, which could clink and jingle as they moved. These beaded dresses were quite intricate and expensive, showcasing the wearer's wealth and fashion sense. In addition, upper-class women sometimes wore sheer gowns of light linen, often ornamented with sashes or capes, and belted at the waist. These dresses were not just practical; they were also a form of artistic expression, revealing much about Egyptian culture and the importance of beauty and elegance.

Jewelry played a significant role in ancient Egyptian attire. Both men and women wore various types of jewelry made from gold and precious stones, such as turquoise, carnelian, and lapis lazuli. The richer you were, the more elaborate and extensive your jewelry collection would be. For example, large collars known as "wesekh" were elaborate pieces worn by the wealthy, signaling their high social standing. Bracelets, anklets, earrings, and rings were all part of this dazzling display of affluence. Jewelry was not merely an adornment; it was a status symbol, a reflection of one's place in the societal hierarchy.

Makeup and wigs were also important aspects of daily attire. Egyptians valued cleanliness and appearance highly, often shaving their heads to combat lice and to maintain a neat look. To protect their shaved scalps and to use during ceremonial occasions, both men and women donned wigs. These wigs could be quite ornate, especially those worn by women, featuring pleats, fringes, and multiple layers. Some wigs even incorporated beads and jewels to make them stand out even more.

Cosmetics were used widely among the Egyptians too. They believed that makeup had magical qualities and helped to ward off evil spirits. Kohl, a type of dark eye paint, was commonly applied around the eyes not only to enhance beauty but also to reduce sun glare. This practice involved drawing thick black lines around the eyelids, giving their eyes that distinctive almond shape. Additionally, perfumes played an essential role in Egyptian daily life. Kyphi, the most popular perfume, made from ingredients like frankincense and myrrh, was so highly regarded that it was burned as incense in temples. Wearing perfume was considered a sign of cleanliness and was believed to have protective properties.

Children's clothing—or lack thereof—also tells us a lot about daily life in ancient Egypt. Younger children, up to about six years old, typically went without clothes most of the year due to the extreme heat. However, they often wore jewelry like bracelets, necklaces, or earrings, mirroring the adults' emphasis on adornment. This practice reinforced the cultural norm that personal appearance mattered from a very young age. As they grew older, children began to wear clothes similar to those worn by their parents. Boys would start wearing kilts, and girls would don simple linen dresses, marking their transition into adulthood.

Clothing in ancient Egypt was modest yet vibrant in terms of accessories. Despite the practicality and simplicity of their main garments, the Egyptians loved color and patterns. Wealthy people could afford colored linens and richly embroidered fabrics, while common folk mostly stuck to plain white linen. This contrast in clothing further highlighted the social distinctions within the society. Even though the basic design of Egyptian attire remained relatively consistent over time, the materials and decorations varied greatly depending on one's social class and occupation.

Moreover, clothing styles were closely linked with their roles and responsibilities. Viziers and high-ranking officials wore long, elaborately embroidered skirts that fastened under the arms and fell to the ankles, along with sandals or slippers. Scribes often sported the simpler waist-to-knee kilt, sometimes paired with a sheer blouse. Priests wore white linen robes as a symbol of purity, and soldiers, guards, and police forces typically donned the simple kilt and sandals, occasionally adding wrist guards.

Summary and Reflections

In this chapter, we've explored the fascinating world of ancient Egyptian children and their daily lives. From their education, which was crucial for their futures, to their chores that instilled a sense of responsibility, these young ones were essential to their families and society. Their games weren't just for fun; they taught them skills like teamwork and patience. And let's not forget their involvement in religious festivals, which helped them understand their cultural heritage and spirituality. These aspects of their lives show how integral children were to the fabric of ancient Egyptian society.

We also delved into what ancient Egyptians ate and wore, shedding light on their dietary habits and clothing customs. Bread and beer were staples, while vegetables, fruits, and fish added variety to their meals. Special foods were reserved for celebrations, reflecting the spiritual significance of food. As for clothing, linen garments kept everyone cool, with accessories like jewelry and makeup adding flair and status. Children often went unclothed due to the heat but still wore some jewelry. Through their food and attire, we see

how ancient Egyptians balanced practicality
with cultural expression, creating a vibrant
and intricate way of life.

CHAPTER 5

Gods and Goddesses

Ancient Egyptian gods and goddesses are like superheroes from thousands of years ago with magical powers and incredible stories. Imagine a world where the sun rises and sets because a mighty deity like Ra sails across the sky in a golden boat, bringing light and hope to everyone. Or picture a powerful goddess named Isis using her magic to heal and protect her loved ones, demonstrating extraordinary courage and devotion. These ancient deities were more than just legends— they were an essential part of everyday life, inspiring awe and reverence among children and adults alike.

In this chapter, you'll get to know some of these fascinating deities, starting with Ra, the magnificent sun god whose daily journey symbolized life and rebirth. You'll learn about his grand temples and the rituals that brought people together in worship. Next, we'll dive into the story of Isis, the goddess of magic and motherhood, uncovering her adventures and the spells she cast to safeguard those she loved. Finally, we explore Horus, the sky god, whose epic battles and symbols of protection captivated imaginations and played a vital role in ancient Egyptian culture. Get ready to embark on this magical journey through the myths and mysteries of Egypt's legendary gods and goddesses!

Ra, the Sun God

Ra's Daily Journey

Imagine waking up every morning to see the bright sun climbing into the sky. For the Ancient Egyptians, this daily event was not just a natural occurrence; it was the magnificent journey of Ra, the sun god, across the heavens. They believed that Ra traveled in a splendid solar boat each day, starting from the east at dawn, moving across the sky, and finally descending in the west as night fell. This voyage symbolized the cycle of life and rebirth, which was essential to Egyptian belief.

The Egyptians saw Ra's journey as a promise of hope and renewal. Daytime, when Ra was high in the sky, represented life, light, and growth. However, when he disappeared at sunset, the world plunged into darkness, only for him to rise again the next day, signifying rebirth. This powerful cycle ingrained in them the belief that even after death, there was a possibility of regeneration and a new beginning, giving them comfort and optimism.

Ra's Worship

Ra was not just a figure of mythology but was central to daily life and worship in Ancient Egypt. Throughout Egypt, grand temples were dedicated to Ra, serving as places where people could come together and honor the mighty sun god. These temples were architectural marvels, often open to the sunlight to connect directly with Ra's presence.

One of the most notable structures was the Sun Temple of Ra at Heliopolis. Here, rituals and ceremonies played a crucial role, involving priests who performed elaborate rites to ensure Ra's favor and protection over the land. Worshiping Ra wasn't just an individual act but a communal event that united the people of Egypt. Festivals celebrating Ra were filled with music, dance, and offerings, creating a sense of collective reverence and joy. This deep connection to Ra through worship reinforced his impact on culture, highlighting how intertwined their religion was with everyday life.

Ra and Pharaohs

In Ancient Egypt, pharaohs were considered more than just human rulers; they were seen as divine beings with a direct link to the gods. Many pharaohs claimed to be the descendants of Ra, using this divine association to solidify their authority and right to rule. By presenting themselves as "sons of Ra," they gained both political power and religious reverence.

This connection was visually depicted in tombs and monuments. Pharaohs adorned their burial sites with images of Ra, emphasizing their bond with the sun god. These depictions showcased scenes where Ra would guide and protect the ruler in the afterlife, affirming the pharaoh's god-like status even in death. By aligning themselves with Ra, pharaohs affirmed the idea that they were capable of maintaining balance and harmony in the kingdom, mirroring Ra's role in the cosmos (Mark, 2021).

Symbols of Ra

Symbols were hugely significant in ancient Egyptian culture, often carrying deep meanings and serving as tools for communication and devotion. Ra, being one of the most important deities, had several symbols associated with him that represented different aspects of life, death, and rebirth.

One of the primary symbols connected to Ra is the scarab beetle. The scarab represents transformation and rebirth, much like Ra's daily journey across the sky. In many artworks and amulets, Ra is shown as a man with a scarab head, reinforcing this theme. Kids can find it fascinating to learn about these symbols because they provide a window into how the Egyptians understood the world around them.

Another key symbol is the ankh, which signifies life. Often depicted in the hands of gods, the ankh looks like a cross with a loop on top. It was believed to bring eternal life and was commonly used in both art and jewelry. Children can engage with this symbol by creating their own ankhs out of craft materials, helping them connect with the ancient culture in a fun and educational way.

Additionally, Ra was sometimes depicted with a solar disc above his head, encircled by a sacred cobra named Uraeus. This image signified his supreme power and his protective nature. Kids can draw this powerful image and understand how this striking symbol emphasized Ra's dominance and watchfulness over the world.

Isis, the Goddess of Magic

Isis, one of the most prominent goddesses in Egyptian mythology, was famed for her powers of magic, healing, and motherhood. Her story and attributes made her a central figure in the lives of ancient Egyptians and continue to capture our imaginations today.

Let's start with the captivating myth of Isis and Osiris. Osiris, the god of the afterlife, was beloved by many but had a jealous brother named Seth. Seth's envy drove him to trap Osiris in a chest, which he then sealed and threw into the Nile River. Heartbroken, Isis began an arduous journey to find her husband. When she finally located him, Seth discovered their reunion and, in a fit of rage, tore Osiris into pieces, scattering his body parts across Egypt. However, Isis wasn't deterred. Transforming into a bird, and with help from her sister Nephthys, she gathered the scattered pieces. It's said that her magical prowess stitched Osiris back together, bringing him to life long enough for them to conceive a son, Horus. This tale highlights Isis's undying love and loyalty, as well as the belief in balance between life and death (Tyldesley, 2019).

In addition to her role as a devoted wife, Isis is celebrated for her extraordinary magical abilities. The ancient Egyptians revered her as the supreme magician whose spells could heal the sick and protect the dead. Her knowledge of magic was greater than that of all other deities, making her a figure of mystery and wonder. Children can imagine how people sought her blessings for health and safety, often invoking her name in rituals and prayers. One fascinating aspect of her magic involved creating spells that influenced everyday life, from crafting potions to protecting homes from evil spirits. Through tales and artifacts, kids can learn about the deep appreciation Egyptians had for the mystical and the unknown.

Isis's nurturing nature also shone through her role as a protective mother. After Osiris's resurrection, their son Horus was born. To keep him safe from Seth's wrath, Isis hid in the marshes of the Nile until Horus was grown and ready to avenge his father. Throughout this time, Isis protected Horus from dangerous creatures like snakes and scorpions. Her image as a caring mother who would go to any lengths to keep her child safe provides a beautiful avenue for kids to relate to the goddess. We can discuss how family and protection were cherished values in ancient Egypt. An interactive way to engage children might be to encourage them to draw or craft protective symbols similar to those used by the Egyptians, such as the amulet of the knot of Isis, which symbolized enduring protection.

Furthermore, Isis played a significant role in the daily lives of the Egyptians. Unlike some deities who remained distant, Isis was approachable, and her worship involved festivals, offerings, and ceremonies. These rituals often formed a part of everyday routines, connecting faith directly with ordinary life. For instance, offerings might include food, flowers, or crafted items dedicated to her shrines. Festivals celebrating Isis were grand events where communities came together in shared reverence. A fun project could involve kids creating their own small offerings or crafts inspired by what ancient Egyptians might have used, helping them appreciate the integration of spirituality and routine.

The temples dedicated to Isis were centers of worship and community gatherings. They weren't just places of prayer but hubs of social activity and learning. People visited these temples seeking her blessings for various aspects of their lives, from good health to successful harvests. These practices underscore the profound respect and love Egyptians had for Isis, seeing her influence in every corner of their lives.

In summary, exploring the story and attributes of Isis offers a window into the rich tapestry of ancient Egyptian culture. The myth of Isis and Osiris weaves themes of love, loyalty, and the mystical, engaging us emotionally while teaching valuable lessons. Isis's magical powers reveal the Egyptians' fascination with the sorcery and the mysterious forces that shaped their world. Her protective instincts invite kids to connect personally with her, imagining the strength and care she embodied for her family. Finally, the role of Isis in daily life illustrates how deeply intertwined faith and regular activities were, providing a holistic view of how the ancients lived day-to-day.

Horus, the Sky God

Horus, one of the most significant deities in ancient Egyptian mythology, holds a special place with his stories and symbols that captivate young imaginations. This section explores Horus's importance, delving into his legendary battles, his association with pharaohs, his iconic symbols, and the temples dedicated to him.

The story of Horus and Set is one of the most thrilling tales in Egyptian mythology. Horus, represented with a falcon head, was the son of Osiris and Isis. When Set, the god of chaos, murdered Osiris, it set off a series of events where Horus sought to avenge his father. The battle between Horus and Set is filled with themes of justice and leadership. It symbolizes the ongoing struggle between order and chaos. Through courage and determination, Horus eventually triumphed over Set, symbolizing the victory of good over evil. Kids can learn about the importance of standing up for what is right and understanding that leadership comes with responsibilities (The Editors of Encyclopedia Britannica, 2018).

Horus is intimately connected with the pharaohs of Egypt. Depicted often as having a falcon head with a man's body, he embodied the living pharaoh. This portrayal wasn't just artistic; it helped establish the divine right of the pharaohs to rule. The notion that the pharaoh was an incarnation of Horus validated their authority, indicating that their reign had divine approval. This concept was so critical that the king's Horus name, which linked him directly to the god, was inscribed on monuments and tombs to signify this celestial endorsement (Mark, 2016).

Symbols associated with Horus are both fascinating and educational. One of the most recognized symbols is the Eye of Horus, also known as the Wedjat. According to mythology, during one of his battles with Set, Horus lost his left eye, which represented the moon. It was later restored by the god Thoth, making it a powerful symbol of protection, healing, and restoration. This symbol was commonly used in amulets and art to ensure safety and good health. Exploring such symbols helps kids understand how ancient Egyptians incorporated these beliefs into their daily lives, wearing them as amulets or inscribing them on important artifacts (Mark, 2016).

Temples dedicated to Horus were remarkable representations of his protective nature. These temples played essential roles in maintaining social harmony and stability. Rituals and ceremonies held in honor of Horus were not merely religious activities but community events that reinforced the interconnectedness of religion and society. For instance, the Temple of Horus at Edfu, one of the best-preserved temples in Egypt, illustrates these practices vividly. Each year, the temple hosted a grand festival where an actual falcon representing Horus was crowned as the king of Egypt, reaffirming the divine bond between the god and the pharaoh (The Editors of Encyclopedia Britannica, 2018).

Understanding Horus's role extends beyond mythological stories and deepens when we look at how he was worshipped. Temples served multiple purposes, from being homes to the gods to centers of community life. Children will find it intriguing to learn that people visited these temples to seek advice, medical assistance, or even to have their dreams interpreted. An example is the practice of seeking protection from evil spirits by wearing amulets of Horus, reflecting how deeply ingrained his influence was in everyday life (Mark, 2016).

Moreover, Horus was not only a protector in life but also in death. He was believed to guard the four cardinal points of the compass, represented by his four sons who protected the vital organs of the deceased. These sons, each associated with a different organ, were overseen by protective goddesses, emphasizing the detailed belief systems in the afterlife. This connection highlights how Horus's protective nature transcended mortality, offering children a comprehensive view of ancient Egyptian spirituality (Mark, 2016).

Final Insights

Exploring the lives of ancient Egyptian gods like Ra, Isis, and Horus has taken us on a journey through myths, symbols, and stories that have fascinated people for centuries. We learned about Ra's daily voyage across the sky, bringing light and hope to the world, and how his worship united communities in grand temples. We also delved into the tales of Isis, her magical powers, and her relentless love for her family, showing us just how deep the Egyptians' beliefs ran in their everyday lives.

Wrapping up with Horus, we saw his courageous battles and his important role as a symbol of protection and justice. His story teaches the importance of standing up for what's right and highlights how the pharaohs were seen as more than mere rulers, but divine figures connected to the gods. These incredible myths and symbols offer young readers a captivating glimpse into the rich tapestry of ancient Egyptian culture, sparking curiosity and imagination about this fascinating civilization.

CHAPTER 6

Amazing Archaeological Discoveries

Exploring the mysteries of ancient Egypt is like taking a journey back in time. There's so much to uncover about this fascinating civilization, and every discovery brings us closer to understanding how these people lived thousands of years ago. Imagine finding a hidden tomb filled with golden treasures or a mysterious stone that unlocks the secrets of a forgotten language. These amazing archaeological discoveries open a window into the past and reveal the wonders of ancient Egyptian culture.

In this chapter, we'll dive deep into some of the most thrilling finds in the world of archaeology. You'll learn about the incredible discovery of King Tutankhamun's tomb, which was packed with stunning artifacts that gave historians a treasure trove of information about life in Ancient Egypt. We'll also uncover the story of the Rosetta Stone, a crucial key that helped scholars decipher Egyptian hieroglyphs after centuries of mystery. Get ready for an exciting adventure as we explore these significant discoveries and what they tell us about the fascinating world of the ancient Egyptians!

Discovery of King Tut's Tomb

King Tutankhamun's tomb is one of the most fascinating archaeological discoveries of all time. Its unearthing has provided incredible insights into Ancient Egypt, shedding light on the daily life, beliefs, and burial practices of this ancient civilization.

The discovery of King Tut's tomb in 1922 by British archaeologist Howard Carter was nothing short of remarkable. Hidden beneath the sands of the Valley of the Kings near Thebes, the tomb lay undisturbed for over 3,000 years. Many tombs in that area had been looted long ago, but not King Tut's. As Carter and his workers carefully removed debris, they finally uncovered a set of steps leading to a sealed doorway. When Carter peered through a small hole into the tomb with a candle, the flickering light revealed a stunning sight: there were golden objects everywhere. This moment marked the beginning of a ten-year excavation project that captivated the world (SHAW, 2022).

Inside the tomb, Carter's team found an astonishing array of artifacts. One of the first things discovered was the famous golden death mask of King Tut—a masterpiece of ancient craftsmanship, decorated with blue glass and semi-precious stones. This mask is perhaps the most iconic artifact from Ancient Egypt. The tomb also contained chariots, thrones, and countless pieces of jewelry, all illustrating the wealth and skill of Egyptian artisans. Each item provided valuable clues about the pharaoh's life and the culture he lived in. For example, the intricately designed chariots suggested that young King Tut enjoyed hunting and riding. The jewelry, adorned with symbols of gods and goddesses, reflected the religious beliefs that were central to Egyptian life (Scriber, 2022).

But who was King Tutankhamun? He became pharaoh at the tender age of nine and ruled for about ten years until his early death. His reign came at a turbulent time in Ancient Egypt's history. His father, Akhenaten, had attempted to shift the kingdom from polytheism to monotheism, worshipping only the sun god Aten. This radical change likely caused significant unrest among the people and the priests. After his father's death, King Tut restored the traditional gods and religious practices. He even changed his name from Tutankhaten to Tutankhamun to honor

Amun, an important deity in the Egyptian pantheon. Despite his brief rule, King Tut's actions helped stabilize Egypt during a critical period. The treasures in his tomb give us a glimpse of his royal duties and personal interests, such as participating in religious ceremonies and learning to use chariots (SHAW, 2022).

The discovery of King Tut's tomb has had a lasting impact on archaeology and our understanding of Ancient Egypt. Before this find, much of what we knew about the period came from other tombs that had been raided or incomplete records. But King Tut's tomb was almost entirely intact, providing an unprecedented snapshot of that era. The artifacts found within allowed historians to piece together details about Egyptian society, technology, art, and religion. For instance, we learned that the Egyptians believed in an elaborate afterlife, where the deceased would need their earthly possessions, hence the inclusion of so many treasures in the tomb. This belief system was reflected in the careful mummification process and the ornate burial practices observed in King Tut's final resting place (Scriber, 2022).

The excitement surrounding the discovery of King Tut's tomb in 1922 also sparked global interest in Ancient Egypt. Newspapers and radio broadcasts around the world followed Howard Carter's work, bringing the wonders of Egypt into living rooms everywhere. This phenomenon, often referred to as "Tutmania," influenced everything from fashion to popular culture. Even today, King Tut continues to captivate new generations, reminding us of the timeless allure of Ancient Egypt.

Uncovering the Rosetta Stone

The Rosetta Stone is one of the most famous artifacts in the world. But what exactly is it, and why is it so important? Let's dive into its fascinating story and discover how this stone unlocked the secrets of ancient Egyptian language and culture.

First, let's talk about what the Rosetta Stone actually is. The Rosetta Stone is a granodiorite stele—a big rock with writing on it. It was created around 196 BCE during the reign of King Ptolemy V of Egypt. What makes this stone extraordinary is that it has the same message written three times but in three different scripts: Greek, Demotic, and Egyptian hieroglyphs. The Greek script was well-known to scholars, but the other two were mysterious. This trio of texts became the key to understanding a language that had been lost for centuries.

Now, let's move on to the exciting part—decoding the hieroglyphs. Initially discovered by Napoleon's soldiers in 1799, the Rosetta Stone caught the attention of many scholars across Europe who were eager to crack the code. Among them was Jean-François Champollion, a French scholar with an intense passion for ancient languages. While others made significant contributions, it was Champollion who finally solved the mystery. By meticulously comparing the Greek text with the Egyptian inscriptions, Champollion realized that the hieroglyphs represented not just symbolic meanings but also phonetic sounds. On September 14, 1822, he famously proclaimed, "I've got it!" and fainted from the excitement. His breakthrough allowed him to read names like Ramses and Thutmosis, bringing the ancient script back to life (Scalf, 2023).

So, why is the Rosetta Stone's decipherment such a big deal in the world of Egyptology? Before the Rosetta Stone, no one could read ancient Egyptian hieroglyphs; they were merely beautiful but indecipherable symbols. Understanding these writings opened a window into a civilization that had constructed monumental pyramids, complex religious beliefs, and rich cultural traditions. We could now read their literature, understand their history, and even get a glimpse into their daily lives through temple inscriptions and tomb writings. The Rosetta Stone thus marked the birth of modern Egyptology, the academic study focused on ancient Egyptian cultures and artifacts.

Now, where can you see this legendary stone today? After its discovery, the Rosetta Stone changed hands several times due to political events. Following Napoleon's defeat, the British Army captured the stone and brought it to England. Since 1802, it has been housed in the British Museum in London. With its distinct black surface and engraved texts, the Rosetta Stone attracts millions of visitors each year, all eager to see the artifact that cracked the code of one of humanity's oldest civilizations (Solly, 2022).

But the story of the Rosetta Stone isn't just about words and translations; it's also a tale of international intrigue. Discovered during Napoleon's campaign in Egypt, the stone symbolized the clash of empires and the race for scholarly achievements. For Egyptians today, the stone remains an emblem of cultural heritage and national pride, sometimes sparking debates over its rightful home.

Remember when we talked about decoding the hieroglyphs? The process was anything but straightforward. Scholars faced numerous challenges because hieroglyphs had fallen out of use long before. As time passed, the connection between the symbols and the spoken language was lost. When scholars began their work, it wasn't simply about matching one word to another. They had to understand the context and nuances, much like figuring out a complicated puzzle (Scalf, 2023).

Champollion's journey toward deciphering the script wasn't a solo endeavor either. Many scholars before him laid the groundwork. Thomas Young, an English polymath, identified that some hieroglyphic signs had phonetic values. Though Young made significant strides, his contribution was a piece in the larger puzzle that Champollion eventually solved. Through painstaking effort, Champollion demonstrated that hieroglyphs weren't just pictorial but worked similarly to alphabets by representing sounds. This epiphany led him to decode entire sections of Egyptian texts, revolutionizing our understanding of ancient scripts.

The impact of the Rosetta Stone on the field of Egyptology is monumental. Imagine if you suddenly found a way to understand everything written in a language that had been silent for over a thousand years. That's what happened with the discovery of the Rosetta Stone. Texts that once seemed like mere decorations on tomb walls or monuments were now readable historical records. Scholars could explore Egypt's ancient laws, stories, and religious practices. It transformed dusty relics into vibrant stories of a civilization that thrived millennia ago.

Why do people flock to see the Rosetta Stone? It's not just because it's an old, important rock. It's because this stone represents a turning point in human history— a moment when we regained access to thousands of years of forgotten knowledge.

Located in the British Museum, it stands as a testament to the power of human curiosity and intelligence. Despite its age, the stone continues to be a source of inspiration and education for everyone who comes to see it (Solly, 2022).

Significance of Archaeological Discoveries

Discoveries like King Tut's tomb and the Rosetta Stone have transformed our understanding of Ancient Egypt. When Howard Carter discovered King Tut's tomb in 1922, it was more than just an entryway to a Pharaoh's final resting place. The artifacts found inside, from golden masks to intricate jewelry, rewrote portions of history by providing tangible proof of the splendor and complexity of ancient Egyptian civilization. Similarly, the Rosetta Stone, unearthed in 1799, played a critical role in deciphering Egyptian hieroglyphs, which had remained a mystery for centuries. This breakthrough allowed scholars to unlock countless other texts and inscriptions, further illuminating the lives and beliefs of the ancient Egyptians.

These discoveries are not just about finding old objects; they offer a window into the past. King Tut's tomb, for example, provided insights into the daily lives, religious beliefs, and societal structures of ancient Egypt. The items buried with the young pharaoh included everyday objects, as well as extravagant items meant to showcase his wealth and status. These artifacts revealed customs related to burial practices and highlighted the Egyptians' beliefs in the afterlife. Similarly, the Rosetta Stone showcased how Egyptians governed their society and recorded their decrees. By comparing the Greek text with the Demotic and hieroglyphic scripts, scholars gained a deeper understanding of ancient Egyptian language and culture.

Preserving these sites and artifacts is essential for future research and education. When King Tut's tomb was discovered, it was largely undisturbed, offering an almost untouched glimpse into the past. To ensure that these treasures can continue to inform and inspire, preservation efforts are crucial. Protecting these sites from environmental damage, looting, and decay helps to maintain their integrity. For instance, scientists now use advanced technologies like CT scanning and DNA analysis on mummies and artifacts to gather more information without causing harm. These methods allow for ongoing study while preserving the artifacts for future generations.

The importance of preservation extends beyond physical protection. It also involves educational efforts to raise awareness about the significance of these discoveries. Exhibitions that travel around the world, like those featuring treasures from King Tut's tomb, captivate millions and spread knowledge about ancient Egypt. Documentaries and books further educate people about these finds, sparking interest and encouraging new generations of archaeologists and historians to continue exploring.

Exploration in Egypt didn't stop with the discovery of King Tut's tomb or the Rosetta Stone. Inspired by these groundbreaking finds, archaeologists continue to search for new sites and artifacts that could shed light on other aspects of ancient Egyptian life. Modern technology has greatly enhanced these efforts. Satellite imagery, ground-penetrating radar, and other advanced tools help researchers identify potential excavation sites without invasive digging. This means less risk of damaging any artifacts that might be hidden underground.

New discoveries continue to emerge thanks to these technological advancements. For example, recent studies using laser scans and DNA analysis have revealed more about King Tut, including details about his health and possible causes of death. Archaeologists have also identified additional tombs and structures near existing sites, each contributing new pieces to the puzzle of ancient Egyptian history. These ongoing efforts demonstrate that there is still much to learn about this fascinating civilization.

Final Thoughts

The stories of King Tut's tomb and the Rosetta Stone show how exciting it can be to uncover the past. These discoveries have helped us learn so much about Ancient Egypt. From the golden treasures in King Tut's tomb to the mysterious letters on the Rosetta Stone, each find has offered new clues about how people lived, what they believed in, and how they communicated thousands of years ago.

These amazing finds make us want to keep looking for more hidden secrets. They remind us that there is still a lot to discover about our world's history. And who knows? Maybe one day you might be the one to uncover an ancient artifact that tells a new story about the people who lived long, long ago!

CHAPTER 7

Fun Facts and Activities

Exploring fun facts and activities about Ancient Egypt is like opening a treasure chest full of wonders. Imagine diving into a world where pharaohs ruled, pyramids reached the sky, and mysterious gods watched over everything. This chapter invites you to embark on an exciting adventure through time, packed with intriguing trivia and hands-on activities that will make history come alive right before your eyes.

Get ready to test your knowledge with interactive quizzes that challenge you to recall what you've learned about this fascinating culture. You'll ace questions about famous pharaohs, monumental pyramids, and other captivating parts of Egyptian life. Once your mind is buzzing with fresh information, you can roll up your sleeves and get creative. Build your very own mini pyramid or craft an ancient artifact using simple materials. Whether you're competing in games that transported Egyptians back in time or constructing your piece of history, this chapter promises endless fun and learning. Dive in and see just how extraordinary studying Ancient Egypt can be!

Interactive Quiz on Ancient Egypt

A great way to reinforce the fascinating information learned about Ancient Egypt is through a fun and engaging quiz. Quizzes are not only enjoyable but help solidify knowledge by prompting young readers to recall facts and details they have read. This particular quiz will feature a mix of multiple-choice and true/false questions, focusing on intriguing aspects such as the lives of pharaohs, the construction of pyramids, and other captivating elements of ancient Egyptian culture.

Multiple-choice questions provide options that guide kids toward the correct answer while challenging them to remember what they've learned. For instance, a question might ask which pharaoh built the Great Pyramid of Giza, presenting options like Tutankhamun, Ramses II, or Khufu. True/false questions can simplify more straightforward facts, helping to reinforce basic yet essential pieces of knowledge. For example, "The Nile River is the longest river in the world: True or False?" These types of questions help kids recall key facts and ensure they engage with the material in a stimulating way.

After each question, answers will be reviewed with additional interesting facts. This method not only confirms the correct responses but also introduces deeper insights, making the quiz an educational experience. For instance, upon revealing that the Great Pyramid was built by Pharaoh Khufu, we could delve into how long it took to build and some lesser-known details about its construction. By supplementing answers with fun facts, we capture the children's attention and expand their curiosity about Ancient Egypt.

To keep the quiz exciting and motivating, a scoring system with pretend Egyptian-themed rewards can be introduced. Kids earn points for each correct answer, which they can accumulate to receive imaginary titles such as "Junior Scribe," "Apprentice Architect," or "Pharaoh's Assistant." These playful rewards make the quiz feel like a game, encouraging participation and a sense of accomplishment. Additionally, setting up different levels or stages in the quiz can challenge kids at various knowledge depths, keeping them engaged and eager to learn more.

Parents and teachers can play a crucial role in enhancing this activity. They can help expand the quiz content beyond the provided questions. For instance, after completing the quiz, they can facilitate group discussions where children share what new information they found most surprising or fascinating. These discussions can spark interest and create a shared learning environment. Moreover, educators can use online platforms like Quizizz, known for their versatile and interactive quiz features. Quizizz allows customization of quizzes to align with specific lesson objectives, providing a rich, dynamic way to cement the concepts taught about Ancient Egypt (ancient egypt Worksheet For 7th Grade | Free Printable Worksheets by Quizizz, n.d.).

Another effective way to elevate the quiz experience is by including small projects based on quiz themes. Teachers can encourage students to research a pharaoh or a specific pyramid and present their findings to the class. These presentations can be simple and age-appropriate, involving drawing, short written descriptions, or even constructing a small model using everyday materials. Such activities foster a hands-on learning approach that further solidifies the child's understanding and retention of the topics covered.

Additionally, educators can introduce follow-up quizzes that dive deeper into various aspects of Ancient Egyptian life, such as their gods and goddesses, daily routines, or monumental achievements. Each quiz could end with a creative task, like composing a story set in Ancient Egypt or designing an artifact inspired by Egyptian art. These tasks allow children to apply their new knowledge creatively, making the learning process both comprehensive and fun.

Lastly, to maintain a lively and engaging atmosphere throughout the quiz, periodic breaks for interactive games related to Ancient Egypt can be integrated. For instance, a quick round of charades featuring famous historical figures or significant events can add a physical element to the quiz. Simple puzzles or word searches with Egyptian vocabulary can also provide a mental break while still keeping the theme consistent.

Hands-on Activity: Making a Mini Pyramid

One of the most exciting ways to learn about Ancient Egypt is by getting hands-on and building your very own mini pyramid! This activity not only makes learning fun but also helps you connect with one of the ancient world's most celebrated achievements—the iconic pyramids. Are you ready to become a young architect? Let's dive in!

Materials Needed

Before we start, ensure you have all the materials you'll need:

- Cardboard: A sturdy base for your pyramid.

- Scissors: To cut out the shapes you'll need.

- Glue: To hold everything together.

- Decorations: Markers, stickers, or glitter to add some flair to your pyramid.

Step-by-Step Guide to Building Your Mini Pyramid

1. **Prepare Your Materials**
   Begin by gathering all the materials listed above. Make sure your cardboard is large enough to create a stable base for your pyramid. If you don't have cardboard, thick paper can work too.

1. **Cut Out the Shapes**
   On the cardboard, draw four triangles with equal bases and heights. These will form the sides of your pyramid. You might

wonder why a pyramid has triangular sides. Well, it's because a triangle is a strong geometric shape and was crucial in helping the ancient Egyptians build such stable structures that lasted thousands of years.

1. **Add Historical Facts**

   As you cut each triangle, take a moment to recall or write down a historical fact about the pyramids on the inside of the shapes. For instance, did you know that the Great Pyramid of Giza was originally covered in casing stones made of highly polished Tura limestone? When sunlight hit these stones, the pyramid would shine like a 'gem'(*Build a Pyramid | TPT*, 2024).

1. **Assemble the Pyramid**

   Once all your triangles are cut out and decorated with facts, it's time to put them together. Apply glue along the edges of the triangles and carefully join them at their edges to form a pyramid. Hold the edges together until the glue sets. Depending on your glue, this might take a few minutes.

1. **Reinforce Your Pyramid**

   To make your pyramid sturdier, you can add a square base. Cut a square piece of cardboard that fits the base dimensions of your pyramid. Attach it to the bottom using glue. This step mirrors how ancient builders might have reinforced their constructions to withstand time and weather.

1. **Decorate**

   Now comes the fun part! Use markers, stickers, or even glitter to decorate your pyramid. Draw hieroglyphics, the writing system used by the ancient Egyptians, or create scenes depicting daily life in ancient Egypt. This personal touch makes your creation unique and gives additional context to what you've learned.

Teamwork Makes the Dream Work

Building a pyramid can be even more fun if you do it as a collaborative project. Pair up with a friend or form small groups and assign roles to each member. One person can be responsible for cutting, another for assembling, and another for decorating. Working together not only speeds up the process but also makes the task more enjoyable. It mimics how the ancient

Egyptians worked in large teams to construct giant monuments like the pyramids.

Displaying and Sharing Your Pyramids

Once everyone in your group has finished their pyramids, set up a special display area. You can use a table or shelf to showcase your mini pyramids. Arrange them so everyone can see the different designs and read the historical facts written on them. This display can be an excellent way to share what you've all learned with family, friends, or classmates.

Moreover, consider organizing a small "exhibition" where each participant explains their pyramid's design, the facts they included, and what they found most interesting about ancient Egyptian construction techniques. This exercise builds public speaking skills and deepens your understanding as teaching others is often the best way to learn.

Final Tips

- **Precision Matters** : Ensure your cuts are straight and shapes are proportional. This attention to detail will make assembling the pyramid easier and the final product neater.

- **Be Patient** : Allow glue adequate time to dry before moving onto the next step. Patience during assembly ensures that your structure remains glued properly.

- **Get Creative** : Don't hold back on decorations! The more colorful and detailed, the better. Think about incorporating elements like sand (to mimic the desert) or small stones to give a real-feel texture.

- **Document the Process** : Take photos of each step or create a short video documenting the building process. This documentation can be a fun way to look back on what you've created and learned.

Creating Egyptian Artifacts

Creating replicas of Ancient Egyptian artifacts can be an exciting and educational experience for kids. By crafting their own pieces of jewelry, such as necklaces or bracelets, they can connect more deeply with the art and culture of this ancient civilization. To begin with, providing templates or guides will be essential. These templates could include outlines of popular Egyptian jewelry designs, like the broad collars known as "usekh," armlets shaped like snakes, or scarab beetle amulets.

To make these replicas, kids will need simple materials such as colored paper, beads, clay, strings, and paint. Each template should come with step-by-step instructions that are easy to follow. For instance, to create a scarab amulet, one could start by molding clay into a beetle shape, letting it dry, and then painting it in shades of blue and gold.

Understanding the significance of symbols in Ancient Egyptian art is crucial. These symbols were not just decorative but held deep meaning. Hieroglyphics, for example, often adorned jewelry and told stories or conveyed protection through specific characters and messages. Scarab beetles symbolized rebirth and regeneration, while images of gods like Ra and Isis represented power and magic. Including brief descriptions of these symbols in the templates can help kids appreciate the cultural importance behind their creations.

Encouraging personalization and creativity allows kids to express themselves while learning about history. Once the basic structure of the artifact is made, let them decorate using their favorite colors or add patterns. This personal touch makes each piece unique, just as the artisans of Ancient Egypt personalized their works. Additionally, kids could be prompted to think about what symbols might represent important aspects of their lives today and incorporate those into their designs.

An excellent way to wrap up this creative journey is by hosting an exhibition. This can be a fun event where kids display their finished artifacts and tell others about the historical context and symbols used in their artwork. Such an exhibition can be organized in a classroom, community center, or even at home with family and friends. Children can set up their pieces on tables or stands, and take turns explaining what they've made and what they learned about Ancient Egypt during the process. This activity can boost their confidence and communication skills, and help solidify the knowledge gained through hands-on creation.

By combining creativity with education, these activities will not only engage young readers but also provide a deeper understanding and appreciation for Ancient Egyptian art and culture. Moving forward, let's explore how these symbols and artistic expressions have influenced modern-day designs and how children can identify similar themes in contemporary art and jewelry.

Ancient Egyptians were master craftsmen who used various materials and techniques to create exquisite pieces of jewelry. Gold was highly valued and seen as divine flesh, symbolizing eternality. Silver, although less common, and semi-precious stones like turquoise, lapis lazuli, and carnelian added vibrant colors and were believed to have protective qualities. Kids can replicate these materials using colored foil, plastic gems, and beads, mimicking the radiant appearance of ancient treasures.

One classic piece of Egyptian jewelry is the wide, collar-like usekh necklace. To create a replica, kids can start with a cardboard base cut into a semi-circle. They can then glue colorful paper strips or beads onto the base in rows, imitating the intricate designs typically found on usekh necklaces. Floral motifs or winged scarabs can be drawn and colored in to enhance authenticity. Explaining to them that these neckpieces were thought to protect the wearer in the afterlife can add an immersive storytelling element to the crafting process.

Another fun project is designing cartouches—oval shapes enclosing hieroglyphs that spell out names or titles. These can be made from cardboard or polymer clay and painted in gold or silver. Kids can inscribe their own names using hieroglyphic alphabet guides, giving their work a personal and historically enriched twist. The concept that cartouches were believed to ensure immortality can spark engaging conversations about ancient beliefs and practices.

Through these projects, it's vital to stress the symbolism inherent in the artifacts. For example, explain that snake-shaped armlets were worn for protection, or that ankhs (crosses with a loop at the top) symbolized life. Encouraging kids to research and pick their favorite symbols to include in their designs creates a meaningful connection between their craft and its historical context.

The exhibition can serve as both a celebratory conclusion and a learning extension. Displaying their artwork not only provides a sense of achievement but also encourages kids to delve deeper into the subject matter. Each participant can prepare a short talk about their chosen artifact, explaining why they selected certain symbols and materials. This peer-to-peer teaching method can reinforce their understanding and make the learning process collaborative.

In addition to individual presentations, group activities can be included in the exhibition. A quiz station with fun facts about Ancient Egyptian art or a craft corner where visitors can make small items like rings or earrings can keep the event lively and interactive. Offering small certificates or awards for participation can add to the excitement and encourage further exploration of history and art.

Ancient Egyptian Games and Puzzles

Ancient Egypt wasn't just about magnificent pyramids and powerful pharaohs; it was also a place where people enjoyed games and puzzles. Introducing these traditional games to young readers not only makes learning fun but also provides insights into the daily lives of Ancient Egyptians.

One of the oldest known board games from Ancient Egypt is Senet, which dates back as far as 3100 BCE. Senet was a popular pastime among children and adults alike. It's played on a rectangular board with 30 squares arranged in three rows of ten. To play Senet, each player has five pieces that they move along an S-shaped path, determined by casting sticks or bones that work like dice. The objective is to get all your pieces off the board before your opponent does. Some squares help you advance while others can set you back, making it a game of both luck and strategy (Hakim, 2024).

Another fascinating game is Mehen, which involves a circular board shaped like a coiled serpent. The serpent's body is divided into segments, representing spaces that players move their pieces along. In this game, players use lion- or ball-shaped pieces and try to navigate these pieces from the outside of the coil to the center. The rules of Mehen are less well-known, but it's believed that movement was based on dice rolls or stick tosses similar to Senet. Despite its mysterious rules, playing Mehen can be a great way to explore the ingenuity of ancient game design (Hakim, 2024).

These games weren't just for fun; they held cultural significance too. Senet, for instance, was more than just a game. It had religious connotations and was often placed in tombs to ensure the deceased could enjoy entertainment in the afterlife. The game's journey represented a soul's passage through the netherworld, making every move spiritually significant. Playing Senet today isn't just about winning; it's about experiencing a piece of history that connected the ancient Egyptians to their beliefs.

Providing printable game boards and pieces allows kids to create their own versions of these ancient games. This hands-on activity can spark creativity and interest in historical crafts. For Senet, you can create a simple grid of 30 squares on cardboard or heavy paper. Use small items as game pieces, like buttons or pebbles, and designate a set of sticks or dice for the moves. For Mehen, draw a spiral on a large piece of paper, and use marbles or small toys as playing pieces. These homemade versions can bring hours of fun while teaching children about the resourcefulness of ancient Egyptian culture.

Encouraging family or group play can further enhance understanding and enjoyment. These games are perfect for cooperative learning, allowing friends and family members to engage in friendly competition while discussing the strategic elements involved. Playing together fosters teamwork and communication, traits that are beneficial both in ancient times and today. Additionally, discussing the historical context while playing can deepen the educational aspect, transforming a simple game night into a captivating history lesson.

Bringing It All Together

We've explored so many exciting ways to dive into the wonders of Ancient Egypt! From interactive quizzes that challenge your knowledge about pharaohs and pyramids to hands-on activities like building your own mini pyramid, you've had a chance to learn and create in fun and engaging ways. Remember, each quiz answer brings new fascinating facts, while building and decorating your pyramid lets you step into the shoes of an ancient architect. You've also started crafting your own Egyptian jewelry and learning the significance behind those amazing designs.

Playing traditional games like Senet and Mehen adds another layer of discovery. You see how children and adults from thousands of years ago enjoyed their time, just like you do now. These activities aren't just about learning; they're about experiencing a piece of history firsthand. So, keep quizzing, crafting, and playing—each activity helps you connect more deeply with the incredible world of Ancient Egypt. Your adventure is just beginning, and there's so much more to explore and enjoy!

Made in the USA
Monee, IL
02 October 2024

67014002R00069